A Heart Of Wisdom

A 40-DAY DEVOTIONAL FOR LIFE'S JOURNEY

OLIVE WILSON

DEDICATION

This book is dedicated to my sister, Jacqueline, who taught me much about life through adventures together and practical advice from her years of experience! Grateful!

Preface

The time allotted to us on earth by our sovereign God is to be highly cherished and celebrated. It is wise to consider the brevity of our days as we make decisions and choices regarding our life's journey.

The purpose of this book is to encourage and challenge us to reflect on the deeper meaning of our existence in the light of Biblical truth. As we view life from the viewpoint of eternity, may we gain *a heart of wisdom.*

If you do not yet know God personally, my prayer is that the truth of God's Word will bring you to a new understanding of His plan of salvation. God loves us all unconditionally and desires fellowship with us now and for all eternity. Be blessed as you consider these reflections and apply them to your life.

So teach us to number our days,
that we may gain a heart of wisdom.

Psalm 90:12

DAY

1

Jesus said to him, "I am the way, the truth, and the life. No one comes to the Father except through Me.

John 14:6

There is a common belief in world religion and philosophy that numerous paths lead to God. Many religions regard Jesus as a prophet, moral teacher or miracle worker, but only Christianity supports the claim that He is exclusively *the* way to God.

A closer look at world history reveals why this claim is fully justified. When sin entered the world, as recorded in the Genesis account, humanity faced an insurmountable problem - sin brought separation from God, resulting in physical and spiritual death. Like metastasising cancer, sin had invaded God's perfect creation. All the blood spilt on Jewish altars could not secure eternal forgiveness nor defeat death.

Before the foundation of the earth, God planned the way of redemption and renewal. The Lord Jesus, the promised Messiah, was born at the appointed time to *tabernacle* among us and reveal God to fallen humanity. His death on the cross was the ultimate sacrifice for sin; only the sinless Son of God could pay for our sins and defeat the power of death in His bodily resurrection.

No one else can save us from our sin because only Christ bore the judgement for us. The veil of the temple into God's Holy Place was split in two when the Lord died (Matthew 27:51), signifying that the way to a holy God was open for all. When Jesus cried, "It is finished!" on the cross, the saving work He had come to do was complete and no one can add to it. No amount of good works or self-sacrifice can atone for our wrongdoing.

The Lord Jesus is the *only* way to God and invites all to accept salvation through repentance and faith. Give thanks today!

Behold, now is the accepted time; behold, now is the day of salvation. 2 Corinthians 6:2

Further reading: John 8:24, Acts 4:1

DAY

2

Stand firm in the Lord.

Philippians 4:1

Where do you stand as you read these words? Atheist? Agnostic? Believer? What shapes your moral and social principles? The *zeitgeist* of today is to question everything and form one's own version of the truth. *If it feels good, it is right!*

This is contrary to the truth embedded in God's immutable Word. The Lord Jesus said: *Heaven and earth will pass away, but my words will not pass away* (Matthew 24:35). God's standards do not change with time; the compass of His Word is an everlasting guide.

The pressure on society to conform to liberal ideology is increasing in an unprecedented manner. Now Christians are losing their jobs for standing up to the gender rights movement; others are being tried in courts of law for staying true to their moral conscience in their businesses. Teachers are being forced to teach inappropriate material to young children in the name of education.

A paradigm shift has occurred in ascertaining what is right and wrong. The prophet Isaiah's words ring out as a stark warning: *Woe to those who call evil good, and good evil; who put darkness for light, and light for darkness; who put bitter for sweet, and sweet for bitter!* (Isaiah 5:20).

Young friends, stand firm in your Christian beliefs and the Lord will protect and sustain you. You may not be the most popular employee, but you will be known in heaven as a faithful servant of the Lord! Those who confess the Lord publicly on earth are acknowledged by Him before His Father in the presence of the angels. This is a greater honour than having favour among your colleagues and the 'in-crowd'. Do not be afraid to nail your colours to the mast in a loving, friendly manner. Stand firm!

"I would rather have the smile of heaven than the applause of the world." – D.L. Moody

Further reading: Ephesians 6:11, 1 Corinthians 16:13

DAY

3

He has delivered us from the power of darkness and conveyed us into the kingdom of the Son of His love.

Colossians 1:13

The Bible tells us that the redeemed have been delivered from the dominion of darkness and translated into the kingdom of God's beloved Son.

While some readers may have been 'translated' at an early age without consciously encountering much demonic opposition, others have been saved directly from the devil's grip. This was the experience of a Macedonian friend, who was gloriously delivered from a life of darkness after hearing the Gospel message twice:

"From my earliest memory, I thought I believed in God, but when I first heard preaching from John's Gospel, I understood that my sin was separating me from God and that it was dominating me. I came home from the Gospel meeting, and with tears in my eyes, I fell to my knees and prayed to God to forgive my sins which were greater than the mountains visible from my window. I realised I was sinful and that Jesus died on the cross for me. He suffered and paid my ransom with His blood as a sacrifice. He procured reconciliation between me and the Father. And so, crying with all my heart and soul, I prayed to God for forgiveness, repented and accepted Christ as my personal Saviour; suddenly I was overwhelmed with relief and joy ... a fullness in my heart and soul.

It was a beautiful moment that I will remember as long as I live, a blissful feeling. I realised at the same moment that God was listening to me. He had drawn close to me, sealing me with His Holy Spirit when I believed. Thank God I am saved from the power of darkness with the assurance of eternal life. Glory to God!"

Likewise, I say to you, there is joy in the presence of the angels of God over one sinner who repents. Luke 15:10

Further reading: 2 Peter 3:9, Luke 5:32

DAY

4

I am the bread of life. He who comes to Me shall never hunger, and he who believes in Me shall never thirst.

John 6:35

Paralympic swimmer, Jessica Long, who has held 18 world records and has been awarded 50 gold medals, asked herself why she still felt empty and unsatisfied despite all her success. She realised only God can satisfy and consequently gave her life to Him in 2013. She would say to other athletes and individuals who have the same feeling of dissatisfaction in life: "It's never going to be enough, but God is enough." [1]

We are designed for fellowship with our Creator. Our spiritual dimension was created for communion with Him through faith in His Son, the Lord Jesus Christ. He is the *Bread of Life*, offering eternal satisfaction to all; when we trust in Him, we will never hunger or thirst again.

St. Augustine of Hippo described those without God's peace as *restless* in his *Confessions*: "You have made us for yourself, O Lord, and our hearts are restless until they rest in you." The innate longing for intimacy with God and peace can drive people to search in the wrong places. Temporal objects will never fill that "God-shaped vacuum" deep within. The cravings of our hearts will only be stilled when we respond to God's whispers of eternal love.

As believers, we do not need to look for satisfaction in the attractions of the world; instead, our whole happiness and peace are found in Christ alone. When we spend time with Him, He draws near and fills our hearts with the steadfast assurance of His presence.

To feel the Master's touch is more precious than anything else we can experience in life. Come to Him today and spend time in the sweetness of His fellowship. He will bless you with His peace and joy as you face the new day.

Further reading: Psalm 107:9, Isaiah 58:11

DAY

5

... And the disciples were first called Christians in Antioch.

Acts 11:26

P ostboxes in various countries are bright yellow so they stand out and are immediately recognisable as such. Of course, the litter bins are also sometimes yellow - it is advised to look twice before depositing letters!

It reminds me of the time when a friend in N. Macedonia was invited to a get-together at another friend's house. What a surprise we received when a police car drew up to the front door! My friend had mistakenly got into a police car instead of a taxi and the policemen were so amused that they drove her to her destination!

Mistaken identity can cause mirth, however, as we examine the identity of the early believers, we can learn from their example. The early believers in Jesus were derisively known as adherents of a 'sect' called "the Way" (Acts 9:2). In the verse above, we read that they were called Christians first in Antioch - the word 'Christian' was employed as a nickname to mark a group that differed from other religions. [2]

King Agrippa, as an 'outsider', employs the term in Acts 26:28 when assuring Paul he was almost persuaded to become 'a Christian'. Peter mentions the word in 1 Peter 4:16: *Yet if anyone suffers as a Christian, let him not be ashamed, but let him glorify God in this matter.* In other words, if someone suffers contempt or scorn for being associated with the name of Christ, they should not feel shame or remorse but bear it for God's glory.

In many countries today, a Christian identity can cause extreme persecution or even death, especially in the Arab and Chinese worlds. Also in the West, especially in Great Britain, it can be a label of disdain in many circles. We should never be ashamed to be Christians but seek to be clear witnesses in our social circles regardless of popular opinion.

Further reading: Acts 5:41, Romans 8:17

DAY

6

The thief does not come except to steal, and to kill, and to destroy. I have come that they may have life, and that they may have it more abundantly.

John 10:10

The subtle snares of this life are becoming more sophisticated and varied because Satan knows his time is running out. His motivation is to annihilate life at any cost and to steal what belongs to the Creator God. Young people are increasingly influenced by social media and peer pressure to behave in reckless ways. The last decades have witnessed a spike in drug, pornography and alcohol use/addiction, as well as a rise in mental health issues, which may sadly lead to self-harming or even suicide.

The solution to this pervasive feeling of hopelessness is to accept the 'abundant life' imparted by the Lord Jesus. The word 'abundantly' in the Greek text is a mathematical term denoting 'surplus' or 'superabundance'. As opposed to the destructive traits of the devil's influence, the Source of Life imparts a new quality of life. The life He gives is everlasting; it starts here and continues in the realm of eternity after death. We can only live life to the fullest through Christ and the abundant spiritual riches He lavishes on us. His wisdom and love enrich and equip us for a fruitful life on earth.

By surrendering our life to Him, we will lose it for its worldly use but will save it for His glory and purpose. Perhaps we think we will lose out on life by embracing radical Christian living, but a life given to Him will never lack His grace or supply. Anything we give up for Him is returned with abundant blessing (see Matthew 19:29).

The Lord's goodness is immeasurable and without end. The Psalmist believed fully in God's lovingkindness: *I would have lost heart, unless I had believed that I would see the goodness of the LORD in the land of the living* (Psalm 27:13).

Further reading: Psalm 34:8, John 1:16

DAY

7

Remember now your Creator in the days of your youth, before the difficult days come, and the years draw near when you say, "I have no pleasure in them".

Ecclesiastes 12:1

The decisions we make in our youth influence the direction of our path later in life. Choices made at the tender age of eleven can determine our educational path and the people who will have an input in our formative years.

Old Testament wisdom exhorts us to remember our Creator in our youth before our minds are filled with the obligations of life. You may be facing decisions concerning your further education, career, future spouse or residential location - as your life stretches out before you, ask God what He would have you do for Him by placing your life on the altar as a *living sacrifice* (Romans 12:1).

Open and closed doors are a litmus test in discerning God's will for our lives, as well as the alignment of Scripture and our spiritual gifts. You may not be called to full-time ministry, but it would be wise to choose a profession which does not go against Christian standards. Many serve the Lord through their faithful witness among work colleagues and by their sterling conduct. Professions can also be used in full-time service such as in the medical field or practical maintenance work; in some countries, a work visa is the only way to obtain long-term residence, enabling missionary activity among the local people.

We can test the wisdom of all decisions with one caveat:

"Unless you are honestly convinced that the thing in question will bring glory to God, then don't do it." - C. Hutson

May God bless your life decisions with His guidance; if some of our choices have not prospered, God can graciously align them to His will and set us on the right path.

Further reading: 2 Timothy 3:15, Lamentations 3:27

DAY

8

Most assuredly, I say to you, unless a grain of wheat falls into the ground and dies, it remains alone; but if it dies, it produces much grain (fruit).

John 12:24

The Creator and Sustainer of all nature understood the principle of a seed dying first to produce a living plant. The outer layer of the seed decomposes in the soil to enable the living embryo to grow and produce more seeds, which in turn yields a crop in fertile soil. If the seed is not sown in the soil, it will remain a single seed.

The Lord Jesus Himself was the ultimate fulfilment of this principle, dying as a Seed to yield a harvest of souls for eternity. Because of His obedience and willingness to lay down His life, millions have received newness of life and forgiveness of sins. This zeal to submit to God was fully demonstrated by Him, our perfect example.

The Lord was also teaching the necessity for His followers to die to themselves in this world. He continued with the words: *He who loves his life will lose it, and he who hates his life in this world will keep it for eternal life* (John 12:25). Paul writes that the old self was crucified with Christ at the moment of salvation, but we must deny ourselves daily. It is only through dying to our sinful, egotistical lives that we can produce righteous fruit by the power of the Holy Spirit in us.

A sincere scrutiny of our motives will reveal if we have truly died to ourselves and are pursuing God's plan no matter the cost. Let us not be discouraged when opposing voices question our motives and commitment.

"But to mean it when I say that I want my life to count for His glory is to drive a stake through the heart of self - a painful and determined dying to me that must be a part of every day I live." - Louie Giglio

Further reading: Galatians 2:20, Luke 9:23

DAY

9

I will lift up my eyes to the hills— from whence comes my help? My help comes from the Lord, who made heaven and earth.

Psalm 121:1-2

It is reassuring to know we are not alone in this world. The Highest of Heaven is interested in the life of every individual, navigating our circumstances to give us what is best. He knows the end from the beginning; He has plans to prosper us and give us a future, according to Jeremiah 29:11. However, we often seek help from God only as a last resort. The Psalmist readily acknowledged the Source of his help in the battles and daily challenges he faced; he was ever mindful to look beyond the hills and ask for help from the throne of God.

There will be times in your life when you saw God's helping hand: suddenly you remembered an important fact in an exam, or that dreaded interview went smoothly, or perhaps you felt God's presence during a critical operation. Assuredly God is *a very present help in trouble* (Psalm 46:1).

During my time as a missionary in N. Macedonia, I experienced much help from the Lord in protection and guidance. One of the shortest, most efficient prayers of my life was when a pack of stray dogs decided to gobble up my toasted sandwich - when I saw them approach, I froze and prayed 'Lord!' At that instance, they stopped barking and filed past me on either side like lambs.

Never will I forget God's power in the moment of need. The same God who closed the lions' mouths while Daniel was in the den can keep us from harm when we cry out to Him. How encouraging it is to know that we can ask God for help with everything. No detail of our lives is too small for Him to overlook. He cares for us as a loving Father and will keep us intact for as long as He purposes.

Further reading: Psalm 72:12, Hebrews 13:6

DAY

10

And what does the LORD require of you but to do justly, to love mercy and to walk humbly with your God?

Micah 6:8

This verse in Micah is a blueprint for godly living. Often in life, we feel wronged in some manner by others or harbour indignation because of a given situation. At all times we are to act justly; we are not to repay evil with evil, as exhorted in Romans 12:17, but to do what is right. Leave the situation to the Lord and He will bless us when we *overcome evil with good* (Romans 12:21).

The Bible tells us that God is rich in mercy and as believers, we are also to *love mercy*. Mercy is an expression of compassion and forgiveness towards someone who deserves retribution. Just as God has extended His mercy to us in salvation, we are to extend kindness and love, even to our enemies.

The parable of the Unmerciful Servant in Matthew 18 depicts the folly of receiving forgiveness while not forgiving others. The king had compassion and removed the servant's large debt, but that servant demanded repayment of a debt owed him by another servant. When the servant was unable to pay, no mercy was shown, and he was imprisoned until he could pay the debt. When the king heard of this, he withdrew his mercy from the first servant.

The Lord ended the parable with weighty words: *So My heavenly Father also will do to you if each of you, from his heart, does not forgive his brother his trespasses* (Matthew 18:35). The importance of being merciful to others cannot be overstated.

The third point in the 'blueprint' verse is to walk humbly with God. Pride is absent from a humble life; our goal is to exhibit the humility of the Lord, who did not exalt Himself but took the lowly place.

"Humility is not thinking less of yourself, it's thinking of yourself less." – C. S. Lewis

Further reading: Proverbs 21:3, James 4:6

DAY

11

For where your treasure is, there your heart will be also.

Matthew 6:21

What does your heart long after? Do you have a deep desire to please the Lord or are you motivated by aspirations of success, wealth, social standing and influence? Christians often have these blessings added to their lives when their priority is to put God first. The Lord taught His disciples during the Sermon on the Mount not to worry about food or clothes because our heavenly Father knows we need these basic elements. His words challenge today's materialistic view: *But seek first the kingdom of God and His righteousness, and all these things shall be added to you* (Matthew 6:33).

If we lay up treasures on earth, they are not shielded from corruption and theft. Deposits to our heavenly bank account, however, are eternally safe and indicate where our hearts truly lie. Contrary to what ancient cultures believed, earthly treasures are of no profit beyond the grave. How we use these treasures for God not only brings blessing on earth but will also have everlasting value. How can we lay up *treasures in heaven*?

We should use all our resources for the glory of God. All that we have comes from Him and should be at His disposal. The apostle Paul encouraged the Corinthians to give liberally, for *God loves a cheerful giver* (2 Corinthians 9:7). Let us faithfully give our portion to God when we gather on a Sunday to support the local witness and missionary causes financially.

We are also to be mindful of the poor. The Bible reveals that God is greatly concerned about providing for the orphans, widows and poverty-stricken people of our world. If we do not know destitute people in our sphere of movement, there are many ways of supporting Christian causes through trustworthy organisations. The Lord will bless our sacrificial giving and give us joyful hearts as we witness improvement in the lives of others. To see human dignity restored to families through financial help is a reason for deep gratitude.

Further reading: Matthew 25:34-40

DAY

12

The works of the Lord are great, studied by all who have pleasure in them.

Psalm 111:2

The first time I ever felt conscious of God was at the age of eight while looking at the night sky; I could literally feel the presence of God while marvelling at His handiwork. *The heavens declare the glory of God, the skies proclaim the works of His hands!* pronounced King David in Psalm 19 v 1. How true!

I did not know God personally, but I knew He was the Creator at that moment and have never doubted His existence since. The night I determined not to sleep until I was right with God was also a night when I looked up into the heavens and thought to myself, "Since the night sky is so beautiful, surely God Himself must be more beautiful!" At the age of eleven, after hearing the Gospel preached, I opened my heart through the working of the Holy Spirit to embrace the Lord Jesus Christ as my Saviour with repentance and faith. The 'works of His hands' and the work of the Cross led me to the Eternal God.

The belief in God and the desire to 'study' His works led many famous scientists such as Galileo, Newton, Kepler, Pascal, Faraday and Einstein to discover facts centuries ago that paved the way to modern science. The verse in Psalm 111:2 is written above the Cavendish Laboratory at the University of Cambridge, a reminder of what has motivated numerous scientists until the present day.

Sir Francis Bacon wrote in his book *Advancement of Learning* in the 17th century: "God has, in fact, written two books, not just one." In other words, God has revealed Himself both in creation and the written Word.

The next time you leave behind the lights of the city, look up into the night sky and marvel at the majestic hand of God - *Lift up your eyes on high: Who created all these? He leads forth the starry host by number; He calls each one by name…* Isaiah 40:26

Further reading: Psalm 8, Psalm 33:6

DAY

13

For his invisible attributes, namely, his eternal power and divine nature, have been clearly perceived, ever since the creation of the world ... so they are without excuse.

Romans 1:20

The littered seashore, particularly after a storm, would suggest a chaotic force at work. However, a closer look reveals much beauty and diversity of design in the natural deposits.

Consider the seashells, for example. Most shells are the former homes of marine molluscs. The soft mollusc has a mantle that absorbs salt and chemicals from the seawater to produce calcium carbonate. Layers of calcium carbonate, which are secreted throughout the lifetime of the mollusc, harden to form the shell. When the mollusc dies, the shell is discarded. The colour of the shell varies, depending on the temperature of the water and the type of food in the environment. [3]

In the 1980s theoretical biologist, Dr Hans Meinhardt, began to wonder how the beautiful shell patterns formed. As he researched, he discovered that the rules which govern the formation of the patterns in nature, such as leaf arrangements, sand dunes and snowflakes, were the same for shell patterns.

The inbuilt mechanism that produces such beautiful, intricate formations points to intelligent design, namely God the Creator. If this world is a product of 'mindless unguided natural processes' as Richard Dawkins claims, we would not expect to find laws of nature which demonstrate such order and regularity in the universe.

Scientists are increasingly questioning Darwin's Theory of Evolution due to sophisticated data from more advanced scientific methods - for example, the complexity of DNA rules out the evolutionary process. True science does not contradict the Bible but supports its claims.

Further reading: Genesis 1-2

DAY

14

Shall the clay say to him who forms it, 'What are you making?'

Isaiah 45:9

The words in Isaiah 45 were a rebuke to Israel for opposing their Creator God; they no longer believed in God for deliverance. *Woe to him who strives with his Maker!* (v 9) exclaims Isaiah.

The warning applies to us today; it is foolish to oppose God and His ways. The Bible states that God made humans male and female, yet this very concept is under attack nowadays, along with the Biblical definition of marriage. While we empathize with people who struggle with gender issues and love them as human beings, we can never condone the aggressive gender rights movement, which is gaining momentum in society today and targeting innocent children.

The Bible asserts we were created in God's image and have been individually designed for a purpose. We did not get to choose our genetic structure, family, country of birth, eye colour, height or gender, however, Psalm 139:16 reminds us that no one is here by chance: *Your eyes saw my substance, being yet unformed, and in Your book they all were written, the days fashioned for me, when as yet there were none of them.*

Do not despair if you think you have no special qualities or if you are struggling with illness or deformity. Helen Keller, who became deaf and blind as a child, famously adopted a wonderful life attitude. Her optimism and faith in God led her to overcome her disabilities and become a talented author, lecturer and disability rights activist.

Living inspiration, Nick Vujicic, who was born without arms and legs, has been used all over the world to speak of God's goodness and the purpose of life: "God is using my life as just one example of how God can use a man without arms and legs to be his hands and feet." God uses those who offer themselves as His mouthpiece – *here am I, send me!* (Isaiah 6:8).

Further reading: Ephesians 1:6, Psalm 139

DAY

15

Therefore, as the elect of God, holy and beloved, put on tender mercies, kindness, humility, meekness, longsuffering.

Colossians 3:12

What we wear says a lot about our character. Bright, bold colours such as red or orange are mostly worn by extroverted, outgoing people while inconspicuous, neutral colours such as grey or beige are predominantly chosen by introverted personalities.

The Bible outlines how Christians should dress; Peter reminds the women to dress modestly in inexpensive clothes as their beauty should be an inner quality. By today's standards, it is difficult at times to find 'modest' clothes which are fashionable, but clothes can easily be altered to ensure they do not cause offence. We should remember to act in love at all times - if our clothing is provocative, we are no longer walking in love.

Metaphorically, the apostle Paul identifies five elements of our spiritual attire: tender mercies, kindness, humility, meekness and longsuffering. We are to be tender-hearted and merciful in our dealings with others while showing kindness and humility. A way of showing humility is to value others above ourselves (Philippians 2:3) and to 'turn the other cheek' when we are slighted or insulted.

Gentleness and patience are also to be worn in our daily walk with a spirit of meekness that readily forgives. These qualities should govern all our relationships - our actions speak louder than words in our witness for Christ. By showing the above characteristics which are rarely seen in our world today, others can be won for the Lord.

Over all these virtues, we are to put on love as the 'bond of perfection'. Love is the outer garment which binds everything in divine harmony.

"Kindness makes a person attractive. If you would win the world, melt it, do not hammer it." - A. MacLaren

Further reading: Galatians 5:22-23, Proverbs 19:22

DAY

16

And those who know Your name will put their trust in You; for You, Lord, have not forsaken those who seek You.

Psalm 9:10

We can put our trust in God in all circumstances. Those who know God's name have this privilege, with the assurance He will never forsake us and that our future is secure.

If anyone knew about trusting God for the future, it was Corrie ten Boom. Born in Amsterdam in 1892, she grew up in a Christian family under the careful instruction of a father who was a skilled jeweller and watchmaker. Corrie became the first certified female watchmaker in the Netherlands.

When World War II broke out, the family began to hide Jews in their home. In 1944, a Dutch informant exposed their work to the Nazis, which led to their arrest the following day by the Gestapo. Corrie and her sister were sent to Ravensbrück Concentration Camp, a camp for 'deviant' women. Her sister succumbed to the systematic torture and squalid conditions of the camp, while Corrie was later released 'accidentally' through a clerical error. Her moving story is told in 'The Hiding Place', a book which I highly recommend.

Corrie went on to write other valued works about her life and mission. She lived a life of faith in God without bitterness about her past, teaching the need to forgive and let God lead in all circumstances. In such adversity, she could say: "Never be afraid to trust an unknown future to a known God."

When the future seems daunting and unknown, trust in the God who knows the end from the beginning. He will lead us all our days and give us the courage to face uncertain moments. *I am the Alpha and the Omega, the Beginning and the End, the First and the Last.* Revelation 22:13

Further reading: Psalm 56: 3-4, Isaiah 26:3

DAY

17

Trust in the Lord with all your heart, and lean not on your own understanding; in all your ways acknowledge Him, and He shall direct your paths.

Proverbs 3:5-6

This verse in Proverbs does not suggest that we abandon our reason and throw careful planning to the wind. If we have committed our lives into the hands of the Almighty, then we are to trust His leading, even when it does not appear to make sense. Our 'own understanding' can sometimes prevent us from stepping out in faith and following God's guidance. Perhaps His plan does not appear to be logical, but He makes no mistakes in His perfect will for us.

Trusting God does not guarantee a level road, but we can be certain of His help and presence on the way. We will have times like Peter, who, on seeing the choppy waves around him after stepping out of the boat, started to sink in fear only to be rescued by the Lord's strong hand. The apostle Paul found himself in many perilous situations, but he could testify to Timothy: *The Lord stood with me and strengthened me* (2 Timothy 4:17).

The purpose of a particular trial or temptation is often only understood with hindsight. We all have many areas of weakness which need to be strengthened; it is in those times we learn to recognize the fiery darts of the enemy and how to defend ourselves effectively. We can have opposition when pursuing God's will - sometimes our families, who may not be believers, do not understand God's leading in our lives.

The Bible is full of broken, human stories made miraculous through the Divine touch of mercy and grace. Peter infamously denied the Lord yet was restored to become a strong church pillar. John Mark deserted Paul on his first missionary journey but was 'useful' to him later after maturing in his walk. Even when we stumble in our path, God renews us and makes the rough paths smooth.

Further reading: Proverbs 4:26, John 14:1

DAY

18

He heals the brokenhearted and binds up their wounds.

Psalm 147:3

The writer of this Psalm was referring to those who had been in exile in the context of this Psalm (v.2). How difficult it had been to *sing the LORD's song in a foreign land* (Psalm 137) and now the bitter memories of Babylon lingered as they returned to Jerusalem. The writer experienced the One who had counted and named the stars as the God who *heals the brokenhearted*. God touched the exiled nation and bound up their wounds to bring healing and restoration.

Broken relationships and marriages cause much anguish in our world today. Couples struggle to balance family, careers, financial pressures, and other troubles which can lead to quarrels and breakups. Others may be facing illness personally or that of a loved one, who may have dementia or a debilitating disease. Some are encountering the trials of grief, having lost a spouse, a family member or a close friend. This is a hurting world in need of comfort and healing.

The Bible reminds us that God is close to the brokenhearted: *The Lord is near to those who have a broken heart, and saves such as have a contrite spirit* Psalm 34:18. In our crushed state, we are usually at the end of our own strength - that is when God draws near and extends His healing power.

We are not left to suffer alone but can bring our wounded hearts to the One who was wounded for us. Not only did the Lord die for our sins, but He also died to make us whole, and that includes setting us free from all that causes emotional or psychological pain.

God's people have been given the Comforter, the Holy Spirit, who knows our weakness and suffering and who *prays for us with groanings that cannot be expressed in words* (Romans 8:26 NLT). As He works in us, old wounds become faded scars which will one day completely disappear.

"He is the Balm of Gilead, the Great Physician who has never yet failed to heal all the spiritual maladies of every soul that has come unto Him in faith and prayer." – J. H. Aughey

Further reading: Isaiah 61:1, Luke 4:18

DAY

19

Be diligent to present yourself approved to God, a worker who does not need to be ashamed, rightly dividing the word of truth.

2 Timothy 2:15

I f you are a young believer with a desire to be effective in your Christian life, it is imperative to have a working knowledge of the Bible. There are no shortcuts to getting familiar with Scripture. You may think you are too preoccupied with pursuing your studies now, but life will get busier in later years as you focus on your career, family and responsibilities.

Now is the time to apply your mind while it is keen and sharp and can memorise easily. There are numerous helps available, including study Bibles, revised translations, online commentaries and dictionaries. Profitable Bible teaching is also offered, not only in local gatherings but also online, resulting from the pandemic.

An expansive knowledge of Scripture keeps our lives in check. C. H. Spurgeon mused: "A Bible that's falling apart usually belongs to someone who isn't."

Not only does Scripture take root in our hearts to bring us to maturity, but it is also necessary to apply its truths when defending our faith. Discussions will present themselves with people of other faith groups, who have extensive knowledge of their own 'holy books'. Believers can testify best by demonstrating familiarity with the Bible and its teachings. Christian apologist, Nabeel Quereshi, who tragically succumbed to stomach cancer in 2017, was strongly impressed by a fellow student when he answered his questions from the Bible, which ultimately led to his conversion.

Since other faiths revere their 'holy books', never place your Bible on the floor or treat it with disrespect while witnessing as it can affect the opinion of your listener. On seeing my study Bible, a Jewish university friend was alarmed that I had written notes on the Torah!

All Scripture is given by inspiration of God … 2 Timothy 3:16

Further reading: Hebrews 4:12

DAY

20

But be doers of the word, and not hearers only, deceiving yourselves. For if anyone is a hearer of the word and not a doer, he is like a man observing his natural face in a mirror; for he observes himself, goes away, and immediately forgets what kind of man he was.

James 1:22-24

I once heard a missionary report on the Middle East during which the speaker pointed out that the practice of our faith in the West and in the East differs. In the East, they practise Christian principles and consequently gain a working knowledge of the theory, while we in the West have an abundance of theory that we often do not put into practice.

When James says: *be doers of the word, and not hearers only, deceiving yourselves...*, we need to pay attention! Hearers only are like those who look in the mirror to check that everything is in place and then rush into the activities of the day without giving another thought to their appearance. A mere looking into the Word and ignoring what is written there does not lead to productive Christian lives. We can deceive ourselves by thinking that basic head knowledge is enough and that if we attend services on Sundays and Wednesday evenings, we have fulfilled our duty as Christians.

Careful study of the Word reveals numerous practical exhortations and commands by the Saviour and the New Testament writers. Passivity does not appear to be wrong on the surface, but James teaches us to the contrary: *Therefore, to him who knows to do good and does not do it, to him it is sin* (James 4:17). While salvation does not depend on good works, James writes that faith without works is dead. The practical outworking involves visiting *orphans and widows in their distress*, as well as keeping spiritually pure. It is our responsibility to put into practice what we read and learn from faithful Bible teachers.

Further reading: 1 Thessalonians 2:13, Isaiah 55:11

DAY

21

**And let us not grow weary while doing good, for in due season
we shall reap if we do not lose heart.**

Galatians 6:9

K eep calm and drink coffee' is a humorous take on the 'Keep calm and carry on' motto of the Second World War in Britain. We marvel at the morale and resistance of the British under the horrific conditions of war, encouraged by Winston Churchill's rhetoric: "Never give in ... never, never, never, never ..."

The Bible also formulates a motto for not giving up in the above verse; we should not become discouraged in doing good if there are no immediate results or rewards for our labour. In due course, the blessing will come if we do not give up or lose heart.

There are various situations in which believers can be tempted to resign. Perhaps you are being kind to neighbours and sharing the Gospel with them but there is no interest in the message; do not relinquish, keep praying for the Holy Spirit to work while being a genuine friend to them. Others may be spreading the Word in gatherings, on the street, online or among university friends without much feedback; continue and do not become disheartened.

The Bible says: *Cast your bread upon the waters, for you will find it after many days* (Ecclesiastes 11:1). We have no way of telling how our witnessing affects those who read or listen; only eternity will reveal the real results when we meet people who heard the Gospel through our efforts.

We live in a day now when street preachers are being arrested, posts are banned on social media and Christians are being accused of hate speech, with the aim of silencing the truth. If there is opposition, it is a sign that our efforts are not in vain. The devil hates the truth and will do all in his power to hinder it; the more he attacks, the more we need to continue and remain faithful to the principles of God's Word.

Further reading: 2 Corinthians 9:6, 2 Thessalonians 3:1

DAY

22

For God has not given us a spirit of fear, but of power and of love and of a sound mind.

2 Timothy 1:7

The scale of tragedies and catastrophes reported in the news nowadays could easily lead us to be overcome by a spirit of fear. We may ask ourselves what the future is going to bring as we face the threat of war, economic instability and rising living costs throughout most of the Western world.

The Bible reassures us that we have received a spirit of power from God rather than a spirit of fear. With His power, we can accept challenging life situations and emerge victoriously on the other side. The power that raised Christ from the dead is the same power in us through the Holy Spirit (Romans 8:11), who gives us new life and purification in our carnal bodies.

In addition to power, a spirit of love should also mark the believer. Paul tells us in Romans that God's love has been poured out into our hearts through the Holy Spirit (Romans 5:5) and that we are to love others as Christ has loved us, even unto death.

There is no greater love than God's love, a love which is sacrificial, infinite and impartial. The Lord was often moved with compassion as He looked at suffering, hungry humanity, providing for their needs physically and spiritually. His unprejudiced love in our hearts breeds compassion and empathy in every situation.

Those who are firmly rooted in Christ have a *sound mind* due to the power of the indwelling Holy Spirit. Our peace of mind is frequently under attack, but we can guard our minds with God's Word, *bringing every thought into captivity to the obedience of Christ* (2 Corinthians 10:5). A *sound mind* is well-balanced and temperate with sobriety and calmness. We are protected from illogical, foolish, rash thinking when our minds are under the control of the Holy Spirit.

Further reading: Philippians 4:6-7, Isaiah 12:2

DAY

23

Though the fig tree may not blossom, nor fruit be on the vines; though the labor of the olive may fail, and the fields yield no food; ... yet I will rejoice in the Lord.

Habakkuk 3:17-18

Numerous self-help books today deal with pursuing and finding happiness. The word 'happiness' is related to the word 'hap', meaning 'chance' or 'fortune'; if our happiness depends on what happens around us, then we will experience changing emotions every day. Habakkuk, however, determined to find his joy in the Lord rather than through outward circumstances. His focus was on God Jehovah, even when legitimate concerns arose.

Like Habakkuk, we can rejoice despite the disasters in our lives by regarding the Lord, the God of our salvation. Paul could also rejoice in the face of suffering and trials: he described himself in 2 Corinthians 6 as "sorrowful, yet always rejoicing" (v. 10) and he could also rejoice in his sufferings for the church (Colossians 1:24).

When we encounter major problems and difficulties in life, our mindset can influence the outcome. The Bible tells us that the joy of the Lord is our strength; remaining joyful and positive leads to victory over the enemy who tries to rob us of our peace and effectiveness for God.

In situations where the devil attacks us through other people's words or actions, we should recognise this as his evil strategy and maintain our joy. This does not come naturally, but it is something we can practise when our peace is disturbed through events.

"Words can never adequately convey the incredible impact of our attitudes toward life. The longer I live the more convinced I become that life is 10 percent what happens to us and 90 percent how we respond to it." - Chuck Swindoll

Further reading: Nehemiah 8:10, Philippians 4:4

DAY

24

And you shall love the LORD your God with all your heart, with all your soul, with all your mind, and with all your strength.

Mark 12:30

The Lord summarised the Ten Commandments into two commands for His followers: we are to love God supremely with our whole being - our heart, our soul, our intellect and our energy - and others as ourselves. Jason DeRouchie comments on this verse: "This means that the covenant love we're called to must be wholehearted, life-encompassing, community-impacting, exclusive commitment to our God."

There have been many examples in history of men and women who have demonstrated whole-hearted devotion by sacrificially giving their lives for the sake of the Gospel. Missionary heroes such as David Brainerd, William Carey, David Livingstone, Hudson Taylor, Jim and Elisabeth Elliot, Amy Carmichael and Mary Slessor, to name but a few, lived inspirational lives - I highly recommend their biographies as challenging reading.

The names of modern-day missionaries are found in prayer guides and various publications. Your contribution to missionary work may not be to go full-time (do not rule it out!) but to pray regularly for those who serve in this capacity. Young person, you can also be part of a team during your holidays where you can actively support evangelism by simply going. Never underestimate how God can use your input and what He can realise for eternity through your availability. You can also serve God wholeheartedly in your profession as an exemplary employee who incorporates Christian virtues, reliability and trustworthiness.

Another way to love God with your whole being is to be a 'pillar' in your local fellowship with a commitment to loving your families and neighbours. The local church needs young people to strengthen the testimony in the area by reaching out to their communities with the message of the Gospel.

Further reading: 1 Corinthians 10:31, Romans 12:11

DAY

25

... You shall love your neighbour as yourself.

Mark 12:31

This is the second commandment summed up by the Lord as part of the greatest commandments. If we love others as ourselves, we automatically keep the section of the Ten Commandments not directly related to God; we will not murder, commit adultery, steal, lie or covet when loving our neighbour.

The parable of The Good Samaritan in Luke 10 succinctly defines the term 'neighbour' - our neighbour is simply someone who is nearby, regardless of race, culture or creed. If that person is in need, we are to help them just as the Samaritan tended to the injured man. In those days, the Samaritans were shunned by the Jews, yet the reaction of this caring man cut across national and political divides. The Lord expects the same of His followers - we are to demonstrate God's love to all people without bias or prejudice.

How we treat others reflects how much we love God; John taught in 1 John 4:20 that if we do not love fellow believers, we do not have the love of God in us. His burning love inside us will compel us to act with compassion. The same love we employ in taking care of ourselves is the measure we are to use towards others, reiterated in the Golden Rule of Matthew 7:12 - *Therefore, whatever you want men to do to you, do also to them, for this is the Law and the Prophets.*

Practical ways of showing God's love can include spending time with the lonely, listening to others' problems, praying with someone and acts of kindness: hospitality, practical help in terms of babysitting or providing transport for those who have no car, mowing someone's lawn, clearing the snow … be creative and attentive!

Another way of loving our neighbour as ourselves is to be genuinely happy for their success and prosperity in life; jealousy is sin before God.

Owe no one anything except to love one another, for he who loves another has fulfilled the law. Romans 13:8

Further reading: John 13:34, 1 John 3:16

DAY

26

And be kind to one another, tenderhearted, forgiving one another, even as God in Christ forgave you.

Ephesians 4:32

C hristians are to be known as kind, gentle compassionate and forgiving. Only then can we tender-heartedly forgive others as Christ forgave us. C. S. Lewis aptly summed up forgiveness in the following words: "To be a Christian means to forgive the inexcusable because God has forgiven the inexcusable in you." We have received unfathomable forgiveness from God for what is *inexcusable* in us only through His great mercy and love.

The Lord Jesus expressed His heart of forgiveness when He uttered the words from the cross in the moments of His intense agony: *Father forgive them for they know not what they do* (Luke 23:34 KJV). As they heaped pain and shame on His crucified body, His reaction was to forgive them, and through dying He extended forgiveness to the whole of mankind.

Throughout history, there have been many instances when humans have publicly forgiven others who were guilty of taking away a loved one or causing an accident in which family members were injured or killed. Brandt Jean, whose brother was shot by a Dallas police officer when she apparently mistook his apartment for her own, displayed an enormous act of forgiveness as he hugged the police officer in the courtroom and said: "I forgive you. And I know, if you go to God and ask him, he will forgive you." Many were deeply impacted by his response. He was later awarded for ethical courage - such an inspiring example!

We are often not willing to forgive because we harden our hearts. When we harbour ill feelings towards others, we place ourselves in a prison of bitterness and hostility. These negative emotions can lead to suppressed anger, which is detrimental to our health over time. We are to forgive as Christ forgave us, meaning the past is forgotten and compassion and love are extended to those whom we have forgiven. By so doing, we honour the Lord and set ourselves free.

Further reading: Matthew 18:21-22, Colossians 3:1

DAY

27

The lamp of the body is the eye. If therefore your eye is good, your whole body will be full of light.

Matthew 6:22

The eyes are one of the most important organs in our body. They begin to form three weeks after conception and are the second most complex organ after the brain. The eye can see millions of colours with a pupil that functions like the aperture of a camera - if it were a digital camera, it would have 567 megapixels! [4]

Our eyes communicate what we are feeling and thinking. Excitement is reflected in wide, shining eyes, while disappointment is visible in lowered, sad eyes. Wide open eyes can express fear or surprise and narrowed eyes can convey distaste - the eyes are truly a 'window to the soul'!

The Lord described the eye as the "lamp of the body". If the eye sees clearly and spiritually, a person's actions will be pure and pleasing to God. If our perception is based on God's light, His goodness will radiate from us, leading others to the Light.

On the other hand, if our eyes focus on what is unhealthy or evil, our bodies will be full of darkness. We need to guard against the 'lust of the eyes' mentioned in 1 John 2:16 in the current visual age. The psalmist prayed: *Turn away my eyes from looking at worthless things, and revive me in Your way* (Psalm 119:37).

In the Book of Hebrews, we are exhorted to run the race while *looking to Jesus, the founder and perfecter of our faith* (Hebrews 12:2 ESV). As we focus our gaze on Christ's life and sacrificial death, we will adopt His character and obey His commands, growing into mature believers who reflect His radiance and light.

Further reading: Matthew 6:23, Proverbs 4:25

DAY

28

As each one has received a gift, minister it to one another, as good stewards of the manifold grace of God.

1 Peter 4:10

I n addition to our natural gifts and abilities, the Holy Spirit has equipped us with specific gifts to serve the Lord. This enables us to do His will to bring glory to the Lord. Every good work that we are called to perform has been prepared for us in the past (Ephesians 2:10); as we serve God, He is working in us to refine us and make us more like the Saviour.

Younger believers may not be fully aware of their gifts or how they can contribute to their local fellowships. Trying various areas may confirm our strengths; not everyone has a gift to teach children or to preach the Gospel, but each of us is gifted in some way to be a blessing in our local gatherings. It is important for the elders to recognise the nature of someone's gift and encourage them to exercise it.

Paul writes about various gifts within the Body of Christ in 1 Corinthians 12: *God has set the members, each one of them, in the body just as He pleased. And if they were all one member, where would the body be?* (v 18-19). Where would the body be without the vital organs which are hidden from view? Much work goes on in the background and if it were to stop, the local fellowship would not function. Those who engage practically are as equally important as the members who play public roles in leadership and teaching.

Find out what your gifts are and look to the Lord to guide you in terms of serving Him. Do not worry about what others are doing, everyone is unique and has something to offer. Ann Voskamp wrote: "Your time is limited – so don't limit your life by wanting someone else's." Be the person God has called *you* to be, a *good steward* of His extensive grace.

Further reading: Romans 12:6-8, Ephesians 4:7-16

DAY

29

He who dwells in the secret place of the Most High shall abide under the shadow of the Almighty.

Psalm 91:1

How refreshing to withdraw under the shade of a sprawling, leafy tree or a canopy on a scorching summer's day!

The Psalmist David tells us that those who literally 'sit' in the secret place of *El Elyon*, the supreme God, will 'lodge' under the protection of *El Shaddai*, the omnipotent God. The 'secret place' is the Father's bosom, the place of intimate communion with Him through the Lord Jesus. It is the place David often resorted to in times of need and distress. In Psalm 27:5 he writes: *For in the time of trouble He shall hide me in His pavilion; in the secret place of His tabernacle He shall hide me...* The inner sanctuary was his place of shelter.

When pressure mounts and we wonder where to go, never forget that God Almighty shields us from the heat of the day. Just as our homes are a safe retreat after a hard day's work, God's presence is our safe dwelling place. American author, Holly Gerth, remarks: "Home is not a place; home is a Person. And He is with us always. His love is the place we can stay wherever we go." We can abide in the shadow of His presence and love.

David also penned in Psalm 32:7: *You are my hiding place; You shall preserve me from trouble; You shall surround me with songs of deliverance.* The 'secret place' is translated as 'hiding place' in this verse, a place where God safeguarded David from trouble. Being in the heart of God's presence prevents the enemy from attacking or hindering us on our way.

When our fellowship with God grows cold and we move away from Him, we are open to temptation and failure, a place of great danger. It is imperative to find time to be in *the secret place* and resort there habitually.

Further reading: Psalm 17:8, Psalm 61:3

DAY

30

Behold, I say to you, lift up your eyes and look at the fields, for they are already white for harvest!

John 4:35

Nowadays we are tempted to leave evangelism to the preachers and missionaries. Each Christian, however, is called to share the Good News of the Gospel with those in their work and social environment. Your workplace can be your mission field as you quietly and consistently uphold Christian values. It has often been said that believers may be the only 'Bible' others will read.

There is a need to meet people right where they are. Paul's missionary strategy is found in his words to the Corinthians: *To the weak I became weak, that I might win the weak. I have become all things to all people, that by all means I might save some* (1 Corinthians 9:22 ESV). When witnessing to Jews, he expounded Old Testament prophecy regarding the life and death of the Lord Jesus. When presenting the Gospel to the pagan Athenians, he referred to their 'unknown god' and their poets, explaining that the 'unknown god' they were worshipping could only be the Living God Jehovah (Acts 17:23-28).

While we must never change the content of the message, we ought to think of intelligent ways to win souls. It is important to listen to the other person to understand which dogma shapes their thinking. Some want to debate Christianity with scientific and philosophical arguments; others may come from a religious background but do not know Christ as their personal Saviour. There is much helpful apologetic material available online, as well as facts about other denominations and churches.

Our goal is not to win an argument but to present the Gospel in relatable terms and understandable language. As we diligently witness and fervently pray for souls, God will give a harvest:

So then neither he who plants is anything, nor he who waters, but God who gives the increase (1 Corinthians 3:7).

Further reading: Proverbs 11:30, Matthew 28:19

DAY

31

Love suffers long and is kind...

1 Corinthians 13:4

The inspired definition of *agape* love in 1 Corinthians 13 is the most profound on record. This love is supreme in value and endurance; no matter what we do for God, if our motivation is not *agape* love, it is in vain.

Agape love is the opposite of selfishness and pride:

Love is patient and kind; love does not envy or boast; it is not arrogant or rude. It does not insist on its own way; it is not irritable or resentful; it does not rejoice at wrongdoing, but rejoices with the truth. Love bears all things, believes all things, hopes all things, endures all things (1 Corinthians 13:4-7 ESV).

It is our calling to share this love in a cold world as a reflection of God's heart; reaching out to others with acts of selfless love and kindness is more effective than we often realise. When someone is touched by God's love through a thoughtful gesture, they usually remember it. God's love will never become ineffective in our witness to the friends and colleagues around us.

God's *agape* love never fails (v.8). Everything else in this world will pass away, but God's steadfast love endures forever. The Father's never-ending love is evident in the parable of The Prodigal Son in Luke 15. How the father longed for the son's return, watching for him each day. When he finally saw him in the distance, we read that he was moved with compassion and ran to welcome him into his loving embrace, despite the son's foolish behaviour. The lavish welcome-home party further demonstrates the depths of the father's love, a true reflection of our Heavenly Father's love for us. One day He will receive us into His eternal presence with the same delight.

In essence, *God is love* (1 John 4:16) and *there is no fear in love* because *perfect love casts out fear* (1 John 4:18). We are loved by the One who *is* love and who has always demonstrated His perfect love towards us. This is the love which motivates and challenges the sincere believer.

Further reading: John 15:12, Romans 12:10

DAY

32

**Each one's work will become clear; for the Day will declare it,
because it will be revealed by fire ...**

1 Corinthians 3:13

Some of the world's architecture is nothing short of breathtaking, from the ancient Pyramids of Giza in Egypt to the Burj Khalifa in Dubai which stands at 828 metres, making it the world's tallest building. These amazing architectural feats reflect the planning strategy, design, skill, time and energy invested in each project, often involving substantial risk.

We are to consider the quality of what we are building in our Christian lives by the materials we are using:

Now if anyone builds on this foundation with gold, silver, precious stones, wood, hay, straw, each one's work will become clear; for the Day will declare it, because it will be revealed by fire; and the fire will test each one's work, of what sort it is. If anyone's work which he has built on it endures, he will receive a reward. If anyone's work is burned, he will suffer loss; but he himself will be saved, yet so as through fire. 1 Corinthians 3:12-15

As believers, we will all appear before the judgement seat of Christ (2 Corinthians 5:10) to have our lives assessed by the Lord. In Bible times, the judgement seat, the *bema*, was a place where the judge awarded contestants. There will be no condemnation before the *bema*, but our works will be tested by fire and rewarded accordingly.

Some will leave empty-handed, having produced low-quality works motivated by selfishness and pride, while others will be rewarded for faithful service. We will have no one to blame but ourselves if we fall short. Let us keep the *bema* before us and build with God-glorifying deeds.

"By and by when I look on His face, I'll wish I had given Him more." - G. Adkins

Further reading: 1 Corinthians 9:24

DAY

33

Nevertheless he would not drink it, but poured it out to the LORD.

2 Samuel 23:16

D avid's three chief warriors came to him at various times in the Old Testament account; this section records their visit while David was at the cave of Adullam, surrounded by the Philistines who were in the Valley of Rephaim. David expressed a desire for a drink of water from the well near the gate of Bethlehem.

The three mighty warriors heard the request and courageously broke through the Philistine lines to get the water, risking their lives for their King. When David realised that they had jeopardized their lives, the water became too valuable for him to quench his thirst with it, so he sacrificially poured it out as a libation to the Lord. He renounced his own desires to give to the Lord in an act of worship.

Another display of earnest devotion is demonstrated by Mary in John 12:3 - *Then Mary took a pound of very costly oil of spikenard, anointed the feet of Jesus, and wiped His feet with her hair. And the house was filled with the fragrance of the oil.* We read that the value of this oil was a year's wages. It is thought that women were given this oil to keep for their wedding day to anoint the feet of their husbands. [5]

David did not allow the chief warriors' hypothetical reaction to stop him from offering the water, nor did Mary hold back from pouring out the expensive ointment or loosening her hair, an "inappropriate" act in this Jewish setting. Such was the outpouring of hearts who loved God first and foremost despite the stigma surrounding these actions.

The challenge for all of us is: how much am I prepared to give to the Lord? Will popular opinion hold me back?

Let us pour out our hearts and lives to the Lord in thankful adoration for all that He has done for us.

Further reading: Philippians 2:17, 2 Timothy 4:6

DAY

34

For I am persuaded that neither death nor life, nor angels nor principalities nor powers, nor things present nor things to come, nor height nor depth, nor any other created thing, shall be able to separate us from the love of God which is in Christ Jesus our Lord.

Romans 8: 38-39

oday's cancel culture means that people who are in the public eye can suddenly be removed from their position due to their views on certain issues - in one day a person's influence can swiftly diminish.

Fortunately, this is not the *modus operandi* of God's kingdom. The apostle Paul faced much hardship and opposition in his life; he was stoned, beaten, shipwrecked, imprisoned and finally executed for the cause of Christ and the Gospel. Yet, in these adverse circumstances, he could pen the inspirational words in Romans 8 that nothing can separate us from God's love. This belief is what gave him steadfast hope to the very end.

God's love never wavers. Human love ebbs and flows depending on emotions and behaviour, but the Source of Love does not change His opinion of us – we are unapologetically loved! His unfathomable love will keep and protect us as we grow in His grace.

The greatest evidence of God's love for us is the cost of our redemption: *In this is love, not that we loved God, but that He loved us and sent His Son to be the propitiation for our sins* (1 John 4:10). The Lord Jesus taught that there is no greater love than laying down one's life for a friend; He went a step further by laying down His life for His enemies!

He sealed the New Covenant of love with His blood, and we rest in the knowledge that nothing will break that Covenant.

Further reading: Song of Songs 8:6-7, Isaiah 54:10

DAY

35

And do not be conformed to this world, but be transformed by the renewing of your mind ...

Romans 12:2

Our mind is attacked frequently by the devil; he has the power to send us thoughts which can subsequently take root and translate into actions. As American essayist, Ralph Waldo Emerson, expressed: "Sow a thought and you reap an action; sow an act and you reap a habit; sow a habit and you reap a character; sow a character and you reap a destiny." How we think will ultimately influence the direction of our lives.

Believers are called to react and think differently than the world around us. Our lives can only be transformed when we bring our thoughts into line with the teaching of Scripture and the control of the Holy Spirit. Our aspirations are to glorify Christ on earth rather than to pursue egocentric ambitions. We are called to overcome the world, the flesh and the devil; as we live out our profession of faith, we will grow in sanctification and grace with the knowledge of God's will.

Memorising Scripture is one of the keys to transformation - in moments of trial or temptation, the Holy Spirit can bring these refining words to our minds. The Psalmist David wrote in his epic Psalm 119: *Your word I have hidden in my heart, that I might not sin against You* (v11), proving the effectiveness of this principle.

When numerous Christians were imprisoned for their faith in Communist Russia, they testified to the sustaining power of the memorised verses of Scripture in their minds.

Today in China, believers receive smuggled portions of the Bible into the prisons and commit them to memory swiftly as they know the precious fragments can be found and confiscated. Strengthened by the Word in their minds and hearts, these precious Christians are transformed as they suffer for the sake of Christ. In our free world today, we have ample opportunity to apply the Word and be transformed in the process.

Further reading: Colossians 3:2, Romans 8:6

DAY

36

His word was in my heart like a burning fire shut up in my bones; I was weary of holding it back, and I could not.

Jeremiah 20:9

Jeremiah's confrontational message from the Lord was not received well in Jerusalem. This led Pashur, the deputy chief priest of the Temple, to make a public disgrace of the young prophet by beating him and putting him in stocks. Understandably, in the face of such opposition, Jeremiah dejectedly decided not to mention God's name again due to the derision and mocking of his hearers. However, the grave words burned inside him and he could not contain them.

It is most difficult to be rejected and disowned by our peers, family and friends. We read of the emotional anguish Jeremiah felt in his tender heart, wishing he had never been born. The public humiliation at the hands of one who represented God's house caused immense inner pain. However, Jeremiah never lost his faith in God and was used as God's spokesman to warn of the impending danger awaiting Israel from the Babylonians.

We should never be unmindful of the plight of our brothers and sisters in countries where preaching the Gospel is illegal. We are exhorted to pray for the many who have been imprisoned as if imprisoned with them (Hebrews 13:3). I will never forget meeting Romanian pastor, Richard Wurmbrand, at our school Christian Union and seeing his scars — he was tortured in prison under Communism for fourteen years for spreading the Gospel. His book 'Tortured For Christ' is a sobering, challenging read.

Let us be encouraged to use our freedom to share the Gospel, even when ridiculed by friends and society. May God's word burn in us so that, like Jeremiah, it wearies us to hold it back.

"Hammer away, ye hostile bands. Your hammers break; God's anvil stands." - Richard Wurmbrand

Further reading: Romans 10:17, Matthew 4:4

DAY

37

But as for you, you meant evil against me; but God meant it for good, in order to bring it about as it is this day, to save many people alive.

Genesis 50:20

J oseph is an Old Testament type of the Lord Jesus; his brothers betrayed him by selling him as a slave into Egypt with evil intent, but God used their actions to realise His plan to save the Children of Israel from famine.

The Lord was also delivered for the price of a slave into the hands of the Roman soldiers, who crucified Him with unspeakable savagery. Yet, God had purposed for Him to die on the cross as prophesied in Psalm 22 and Isaiah 53. While being 'put to death', the Lord willingly laid down His life to save us from our sins and eternal judgement. God, in His sovereignty, incorporates the rebellion of man into His purposed will and brings good out of man's wicked schemes.

We would be naïve if we thought everyone was for us. There are now evil forces at work on the world stage which are aggressively attacking God's order of nature with anti-Christian rhetoric and actions. However, God protects those targeted. In the Old Testament, the battle plans of the enemies of Israel were often thwarted by the Living God (see Exodus 14:23-25, Isaiah 8:10).

The Psalmist wrote in Psalm 124: *"If it had not been the Lord who was on our side,"* let Israel now say - *"If it had not been the Lord who was on our side, when men rose up against us, then they would have swallowed us alive, when their wrath was kindled against us..."* (v1-3).

Take courage if you encounter opposition; if others set out to harm you physically or with slander, God can turn it around and bring good out of the situation (Romans 8:28). The truth will vindicate you if you let God work instead of seeking revenge (Romans 12:19).

Further reading: Luke 6:27-28, Romans 12:14

DAY

38

I am ready to perform My word.

Jeremiah 1:12

When almond blossoms appear, we know spring is near; how beautiful are the delicate, fragrant flowers!

In Jeremiah chapter 1, we read of a conversation between the young prophet Jeremiah and God. God asks Jeremiah what he sees, and he replies: *"I see a branch of an almond tree"* (Jeremiah 1:11). The LORD replies: *"You have seen well, for I am ready to perform My word"* (v 12).

The word for 'almond tree' in Hebrew is derived from the word for 'watchful'. The play on words is lost in the English translation, but it becomes clear when the Hebrew is highlighted: "The 'almond tree' is *saqed* and God is 'watching' (*soqed*) over his word to fulfil it." (Feinberg). [6]

As we witness the horror of current events such as wars, mass shootings and persecution, we could easily become discouraged and depressed. We could justifiably wonder where God is in all this mayhem and ask why He appears to be silent. Why does He permit such suffering? Why does He not intervene to stop the evil?

There is no easy answer to these questions. As we pray with heavy hearts for our world, let us remember that our Sovereign God is watching, and He hears the prayer of the righteous: *For the eyes of the Lord are on the righteous, and His ears are open to their prayers; but the face of the Lord is against those who do evil.* (1 Peter 3:12)

Just as the almond blossoms appear after the long winter as a sign of the coming spring, we are assured that God is watching over His word and will fulfil it in His appointed time.

Further reading: Matthew 24:35-36, Matthew 5:18

DAY

39

Therefore you also be ready, for the Son of Man is coming at an hour you do not expect.

Matthew 24:44

Only our Father in Heaven knows when the Second Coming of the Lord Jesus will take place. What is certain is His *soon* return due to the signs already happening in our world today.

In the end-time discourse of Matthew 24:7-8, the Lord mentioned the signs: *For nation will rise against nation, and kingdom against kingdom, and there will be famines and earthquakes in various places. All these are but the beginning of the birth pains* (ESV). We have seen these *birth pains* intensify over the last decades; surely His coming is very near!

The Second Coming will be in two stages; first, the Lord will come to the air for the Church as recorded in 1 Thessalonians 4:16-17 - *For the Lord Himself will descend from heaven with a shout, with the voice of an archangel, and with the trumpet of God. And the dead in Christ will rise first. Then we who are alive and remain shall be caught up together with them in the clouds to meet the Lord in the air. And thus we shall always be with the Lord.*

There is nothing to be fulfilled in Scripture for this to happen. It could happen today or in several years' time, but the imperative for us is to be ready. The Bible mentions that He will *come like a thief in the night* (Matthew 24:43).

Once the Church has been raptured and the *Restrainer* removed (2 Thess. 2:7), the anti-Christ will be revealed and will rule for a seven-year period known as the Great Tribulation. He will deceive the nations and promise world peace, which will materialize for three-and-a-half years. The latter three-and-a-half-year period will be a time of great trouble and distress, culminating in the Battle of Armageddon. This will be the second stage of the Lord's coming when He will defeat the anti-Christ and will set up His millennial reign on the earth. *Maranatha!*

Further reading: 1 Thessalonians 5:2, Zechariah 12:10

DAY

40

Now may the God of hope fill you with all joy and peace in believing, that you may abound in hope by the power of the Holy Spirit.

Romans 15:13

The Christian life is one of hope, joy and peace because of the God of hope who leads and guides us. We often hear optimistic phrases in common speech such as 'we can only hope for the best' or 'I hope it turns out well', without any guarantee of the result. Hope in the Bible, however, is not wishful thinking; the word 'elpis' in Greek means a sure confidence that what has been promised will come to pass. The hope of the believer is derived from a God who cannot lie or renege on His promises.

Writer S. Hafemann's definition of hope sheds further light on the subject: 'Hope in God's promises, therefore, is not a wishful longing but a faith-filled confidence for the future. It is simply impossible to trust one of God's promises and not anticipate its coming true. To know God is to trust Him. And to trust God is to trust His promises. And to trust God's promises is to be sure of their fulfillment. This assurance concerning the future, anchored in God's promises, is what the Bible calls "hope."'

Christian hope comes through the power of the Holy Spirit. Paul's wish for the Roman believers was that they may 'superabound' or overflow in hope. This is possible by the empowerment of the Holy Spirit in our minds and hearts.

In a world full of fear and uncertainty, believers can remain joyful and at peace through God's divine hope. His hope and joy will lead us home. *For You are my hope, O Lord God; You are my trust from my youth* (Psalm 71:5).

Further reading: Romans 8:24-25, 1 Peter 1:3

REFERENCES

1. cbnnews.com: "Paralympian Jessica Long Had 50 Gold Medals but No Peace, Then She Gave Her Heart to Jesus: 'God Is Enough'" — Will Dawson

2. Elliot's Commentary for English Readers (biblehub.com)

3. https://sciencing.com/how-seashells-formed-4923554.html

4. https://www.advvisioncenters.com/eye-health/insane-facts-about-eyes/

5. https://bibletruthpublishers.com/love-returned/women-of-the-new-testament-july-2021/the-christian/la178554

6. https://enduringword.com/bible-commentary/jeremiah-1/

*Some things need
time to ripen.
Be patient!*

Take my life and let it be
consecrated, Lord, to thee.
Take my moments and my days;
let them flow in ceaseless praise.

Take my hands and let them move
at the impulse of thy love.
Take my feet and let them be
swift and beautiful for thee.

Take my silver and my gold;
Not a mite would I withhold;
Take my intellect and use
Every power as Thou shalt choose.

Take my will and make it Thine;
It shall be no longer mine.
Take my heart; it is Thine own;
It shall be Thy royal throne.

F. R. Havergal

*Your potential is
the sum of all the
possibilities God
has for your life.*

C. Stanley

OTHER PUBLICATIONS

Surrounded By Beauty – Pictures of Cyprus with 40 Encouraging Bible Verses

Available on Amazon, hardcover, paperback and Kindle editions.

Printed by Amazon Italia Logistica S.r.l.
Torrazza Piemonte (TO), Italy